Contents

Why did people build castles?

Castles were built a long time ago.

They were built for the king and his lords to keep them and their families safe. They ordered the peasants to build the castles for them.

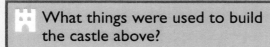
What things were used to build the castle above?

First, the peasants chopped down some trees to build a wooden fence. This was called a **palisade**.

The space inside the palisade was called a **bailey**.

Outside the fence they dug a ditch to keep unwanted people out. This ditch is called a **moat**.

They used the soil from the ditch to make a big hill inside the ditch. This was called a **motte**.

On top of the motte they built a wooden **keep**. This was for the lord to live in.

# ow were castles made stronger?

The wooden tower was knocked down and a stone one was built in its place. This tower was much bigger. It was called a keep.

The wooden fence was also pulled down. In its place they built a tall stone wall. This was called a **curtain wall**. It was often wide enough for soldiers to walk along the top. On it were **battlements** that soldiers hid behind when they fired arrows.

Later on, square towers were added to the curtain wall to stop people trying to knock it down. This made the castle even stronger.

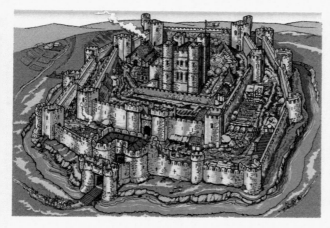

Some castles had an extra wall around them. This made it even harder for attackers to get inside.

They also had round towers. These were much stronger than square towers.

 How did the castles on these two pages keep people safe?

ho lived in castles?

This is my castle. I have many more in other parts of the country.

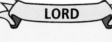
LORD

I am in charge of the soldiers and make sure the castle is safe.

CONSTABLE

I look after all the horses and carts.

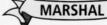
MARSHAL

SOLDIERS

The lord and his family lived in the castle with many soldiers and servants.

We defend the castle and protect the lord when he travels around.

I look after our children and attend my lord when he needs me.

The lord's wife and her servants were the only women who lived in the castle. The other women lived in villages nearby.

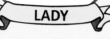

LADY

I look after the lord's rooms and all his belongings. I also look after his clothes.

I am in charge of the household servants.

CHAMBERLAIN

STEWARD

We are too busy to stop and tell you what we do. There is so much work to be done around here.

SERVANTS

 How are clothes of these people different to your clothes?

 # hat was it like inside a castle?

The lord and his family lived on their own at the top of the keep.

They had the best rooms and were looked after by servants. Life was very comfortable for them.

 How many objects in this picture do we still use today?

The great hall was the main room of the castle.
Each morning the important servants met here.

They talked about and planned all the work that
needed doing around the castle.

 How many different activities can
you see in this picture?

In the kitchen the servants are busy.

They have a lot of work to do to make the evening meal.

 What jobs are the servants doing in this picture?

On top of the curtain wall soldiers keep a look out around the bailey.

Down below other soldiers practise using their weapons. Nearby, men are looking after the horses.

 What are all the people doing in the bailey?

At the end of the day everyone went to the great hall. They ate their evening meal together.

After the meal it was time for bed. The lord and his family slept in their own rooms.

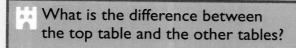
What is the difference between the top table and the other tables?

The most important servants had rooms in the castle's towers. The other servants slept anywhere they could. The soldiers slept on the floor of the great hall on mattresses.

Before going to bed some people needed to go to the **garderobe**. Other people went to the chapel to say prayers. The prisoner locked up in the dungeon could go nowhere.

 How different are the places where people slept?

How did attackers try to get inside castles?

Attackers used many different ways to get inside the castle. They tried to break down the main gate or smash a hole in the curtain walls. Some attackers tried to climb over the walls. Others dug a tunnel underneath.

Can you find these objects in the picture?
Scaling ladder, catapult, siege tower and **battering ram.**

 # ow were attackers kept out of castles?

This is how people inside the castle stopped attackers from getting inside.

Shooting arrows
at attackers.

Lifting the
drawbridge to keep
the enemy out.

Dropping hot water through holes in the battlements.

Throwing rocks that bouned off the **plinth.**

hy were castles no longer used?

As the country became more peaceful there was less fighting. People no longer needed to live in castles.

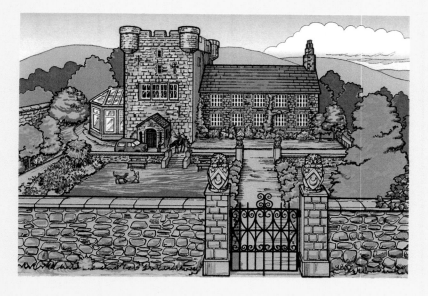

Some lords made their castles into comfortable homes. They added new parts to them. They also made nice gardens around their castles.

> What has been done to make the castle above a more comfortable place to live in?

Other lords moved out of their castles and built large new houses nearby.

They let their castles fall into ruin.

This castle is now looked after by English Heritage. You can come to visit the castle and walk round the ruins.

 Which parts of the ruined castle are missing, and why?

Glossary

Here are some of the key words you've learnt.
These words can be found in bold in the text.

bailey
The area inside the palisade. This is where the castle buildings stand.

battering ram
A large, heavy log used for smashing through the drawbridge.

battlements
The low wall at the top of a castle that has spaces to allow soldiers
to fire through at invaders.

catapult
A weapon used for throwing missiles at the enemy.

curtain wall
A big, stone wall that is built around the castle to protect it
from attack.

drawbridge
A bridge that can be raised or lowered to allow people in
and out of the castle.

garderobe
The castle toilet.